Eddie Thompson

POETRY
Sweet & Sour

Another collection of verses

mereo

Mereo Books

2nd Floor, 6-8 Dyer Street, Cirencester, Gloucestershire, GL7 2PF
An imprint of Memoirs Book Ltd. www.mereobooks.com

POETRY SWEET AND SOUR

978-1-86151-968-9

First published in Great Britain in 2020
by Mereo Books, an imprint of Memoirs Books Ltd.

The address for Memoirs Books Ltd. can be
found at www.memoirspublishing.com

Memoirs Books Ltd. Reg. No. 7834348

Typeset in 11/15pt Bembo
by Wiltshire Associates Ltd.
Printed and bound in Great Britain

INTRODUCTION

These verses won't lift you,
They haven't the magic of self-raising flour
As I said to my wife,
They echo life,
Some are sweet and some are sour.

ABOUT THE AUTHOR

I asked the author, "What shall we put here?"
And I have to tell you that he bent my ear,
So we're following his instructions, to the letter,
"The less they know," he said, "the better".

ALSO BY EDDIE THOMPSON

Poetry Lite
Poetry Free Range
Poetry Decaffed
Poetry Semi-Skimmed
Poetry Plain
Poetry Unsalted

DEDICATION

To those who helped, or offered, or asked about our health
During the Covid-19 pandemic, I dedicate this book with
thanks, for in you all lies our wealth.

CONTENTS

SHORT ONES

Radio operators are told everywhere,
Be precise, be brief, then get off the air,
And as they say, old habits die hard,
So verses over five lines are barred.

SHORT ONES
CONTENTS

FOCUS

We all need something to focus on,
Without that things can go wrong.
Without a clear focus boredom grinds,
And slowly produces stultified minds.

DIFFICULT RULES

Two rules told me by my mother,
Both difficult to adhere to,
Both difficult guides to steer to:
Avoid the word hate and love one another.

THE GREAT LINFORD COMMUNITY FRIDGE

Come one come all and forage in the fridge,
Between waste and want they have built a bridge.

PURITANS

So many people are still puritanical,
Is this a good thing or bad?
Each to his own but they do sound tyrannical,
And Puritans, we read, were seriously sad.

A MODERN DAY
KNIGHT ERRANT

In the pantheon of super-heroes, that's where he belongs,
I speak of course of that indomitable righter of wrongs,
That example of the übermensch, so beloved by Nietzsche,
That ex US army policeman, Major Jack (none) Reacher.

SCHOOLDAYS

School was not a pleasant place,
School I fear was violent,
One slap across the face,
Then the class fell silent.

A WILD GOOSE CHASE

Why this silly search for perfection?
When none of us bear a close inspection.

"ESMERALDA HAS SOMETHING FOR YOU"

My inbox is being bombarded,
And sometimes I'm tempted to see,
Just what it is exactly,
That Esmeralda has for me.

FIRST IMPRESSIONS

Don't be quick to judge should you see no surface shine,
There's so much more to all of us below the Plimsoll Line.

GOOD POSTURE

Good posture the blues will scatter,
That's what good posture's about,
So lift your chin up and throw your chest out
(Enid refuses to do the latter).

ANSWERS PLEASE

My disbeliefs a Christian would appal,
So am I indeed a Christian at all?

FASHION 2

Some pages I avoid with a passion,
Horse racing and sartorial fashion.

WHAT A LET DOWN

Breast implants were installed,
But the lady was left appalled,
Disappointed, totally up-ended,
The procedure went pear-shaped, no pun intended.

THE HUMAN HERON

He stands still for days and never complains,
The cricket umpire, with varicose veins.

JOLLY VERSES WANTED

Would I read my verses at a family party?
Of course, but with verses hale and hearty?
This is going to be hard to do,
For of that sort of verse I have but a few.

SOMETHING WE ALL HAVE

Friends, strangers, all have a history,
That's the attraction, the aura of mystery.

SO I'M NOT ALONE

There's a certain realization that the ageing process brings,
The reassuring knowledge that we ALL do stupid things.

HELP!

It's the weirdest 'chat-up' line I've ever heard,
"Where do you stand on transubstantiation?"
Clearly a nerd, interesting, but still a nerd,
I shrugged my shoulders and asked for a translation.

A STATISTIC WE WILL NEVER KNOW

How many of us are, I wonder,
An unintended consequence?
The result of a one-night lusty blunder,
And a failure to observe due diligence.

LET'S HEAR IT FOR PRUNES

To prunes and prune juice I am in debt,
For as laxatives go, they're the best I can get,
They ease the strain, make it less of a tussle,
And exercise the sphincter muscle.

A ROUND BUNG IN
A ROUND HOLE

Why do men stand with their bums to a fire?
'Cos the Ark sprung a leak, much to Noah's ire,
Noah sat on the leak, thus saving the hold,
Ever since then men's bums have been cold.

HOARDER OR ACTIVIST?

Enid, my wife, calls me a hoarder,
As recording events I can't resist,
And because they're filed strictly in order,
Friend Noel calls me an archivist.

EQUAL RIGHTS

Equal Rights, will we ever see it?
Will those in power ever agree it?
Women are right as they seek, (and not as a perk),
Equal pay for equal work.

IRON AGED

Low blood pressure? Headaches? Then iron is a must,
That's all very well, but will I rust?

THIS CAN HAPPEN WHEN THEY'RE OUT THERE

I like the short ones best,
Said an acquaintance, at no one's request.
Curious, I asked him why,
He ignored my question and walked on by.

BUT THE TAIL CAN SOMETIMES WAG

Using cricket as a metaphor for life,
I'm a tail-ender, unlike Enid my wife.

IT WON'T BE ENOUGH

When gate-keeper Peter
The Pearly Gate unlocks,
I'll ingratiate the greeter
By wearing Holy socks.

LIMERICKS

Introduction

Limericks are not always bawdy and rude,
Take this one, it can't be said that it's crude,
And after all is said and done,
They're just a bit of puerile fun.
Nevertheless, they're not enjoyed by the strait-laced prude.

LIMERICKS

CONTENTS

PEEL

My City of Dreams I will now reveal,
Surprise surprise, it has to be Peel (look it up),
Its cathedral and castle,
And complete lack of hassle,
Along with its kippers, make Peel the real deal.

A KINDLY OLD CODGER
FROM WAREHAM

A kindly old codger from Wareham,
Was asked, "Are you keeping a harem?"
He said, "Yes indeed,
And if you're in need,
For a fee I am willing to share 'em."

ANCHORITES

Unwashed nuts,
In primitive huts,
Anchorites, seeking isolation,
After some consideration,
They must have been bonkers, with amoebic guts.

"I'M REVIEWING THE SITUATION"

I'm sitting on the toilet, contemplating
Our strange situation consolidating,
Enid and I are in total lockdown,
At our age this is running the clock down,
Our freedoms this virus is confiscating.

LENT

I know what to give up for Lent,
Writing poetry with lewd intent.
My verse will have a clean bill of health,
No inserting smut by stealth,
Self-censorship I'll implement.

THERE WAS A YOUNG MAN FROM BUDE

There was a young man from Bude
Who wrote limericks, puerile and lewd,
About people he knew,
They were all untrue,
They all took umbrage and sued.

LISTEN, SAID LILY FROM LEEDS

Listen, said Lily from Leeds,
No one ever succeeds,
Without a bit,
Of Yorkshire grit,
So man-up please, she pleads.

A RIGHT ROYAL FLUSH

An acquaintance with acute constipation,
After serious contemplation,
Took yogurt and prunes for almost a week,
The result of which I can barely speak,
A volcanic colonic evacuation.

THE BUCKET LIST

The time has come, I really ought,
To write a bucket list, I thought,
But pretty soon my heart did sink,
Of things to do I could not think,
And now, of time I'm running short.

HE KNELT BEFORE THE PEARLY GATES

He knelt before the Pearly Gates, God's Mansion to enjoy,
But know this, he had form, let us not be coy,
Then from Peter, Keeper of the Keys,
'Get up my son, get up off your knees,
For you are barred, he said, you were a very naughty boy'.

SAINT BENJAMIN

Make him the Patron Saint of our grateful nation,
For his name invokes courage and dedication,
Bow down before him,
Worship and adore him,
Give to Ben Stokes our veneration.

August 2019

JUST OCCASIONALLY

Occasionally our fires (boilers, energy) need stoking,
Our egos need stroking,
Support invoked,
Consciences provoked,
You know this is true, you know I'm not joking.

ANOTHER FIVE LIMERICKS

There was a young woman called Sandra,
Who fell for a guy from Uganda,
To wed she was enticed,
And at Gretna they were spliced,
But he turned out to be a philanderer.

I read of the revival of Manx,
And the many that are swelling their ranks,
How great that they're willing to strive,
At keeping the language alive,
To them all go my heartfelt thanks.

For some time now I have felt
Satisfied with the hand I've been dealt,
This deal can't be gazumped,
This card cannot be trumped,
I thank the dealer I'm a Celt.

Diarists display a persistence,
More than that, an insistence,
To record delights that they've tasted,
And/or opportunities wasted,
In their day-to-day existence.

Huw Pugh Bartholomew,

Would burst into song when he'd had a few,

He'd sing bits and pieces, this and that,

Hymns and arias, mostly flat,

But the whole pub would follow Huw.

PREPARATION POSTPONED

We must declutter, En said,

For t'wont be long 'till we're dead.

Now that we're toothless,

We should be ruthless,

And those love-letters we should shred.

Hold on a moment, said Ed,

Decluttering is something I'll dread,

Don't be so fast,

This 'stuff' is our past,

Look! This is the day we were wed.

They sat down and gave it some thought,

And agreed that to do it they ought,

Their minds they then set,

But not just yet,

Ed's state of mind En had caught.   August 2019

WHY ARE WE HERE?

Whatever, but here we are,
Holding tight 'till we "cross the bar",
Carried on life's ebb and flow,
Sustained by our spark's inner glow,
Shepherded, perhaps, by a guiding star.

SIX-LINERS

These six-liners, 'sixains' in the trade,
(It's a word I've never heard before,
So to use it I'm afraid),
Are short, too short to bore,
Though poetry purists may be appalled,
Six-liners they're going to be called.

SIX LINERS

CONTENTS

The Bullingdon Club
Cousin Frances
A Teasel to Talk About
Worried? Me?
Would you believe it!
On Trial
A Whole New Lexicon
Standing up to the Coronavirus
"Through Fair or Frosty Weather"
Bewitched
A Delicacy (for some)
"Fat People are Harder to Kidnap"
It's Make Your Mind Up Time
Dissonance
Food and Sex
Currently on Remand
Captivated
A Quartet
Infidelity
Judges Chapter16 v 16
It's July 2020
Alcohol, Narcotics, Power, Beauty etc
Who or What Inspired you to Write?
The Day After Tomorrow

FITTING IN

Our downstairs loo has a bigger pan and sink,
Which means you can bang your knees,
It's smaller than you think.
The reign of avocado green has ended,
'Though now it is a tight squeeze,
(No pun intended).

THIS IS GETTING UP MY NOSE

Every time I leave the house,
I am inspected by my spouse,
It's not to check that I'm properly dressed,
It's my nose, my nose, with which she's obsessed.
Each time she tells me, on my oath,
It's either hairy, wet or both.

SHOULD I BE WORRIED?

My swollen lips are ruby red,
So something's not quite right
I wonder, would a day in bed,
Help rid this worrying sight?
My wife suggests a paler hue,
"Ruby red dear, isn't you".

MY LOWER LIP IS STILL SWELLING

My lower lip is swelling,

(Please note the alliteration),

In cordial conversation,

It seems compulsory, certainly compelling,

To tell me that my lower lip is bulging,

Then to ask, in what am I indulging?

June '20

YOGA

For Enid and me a new phase is dawning,

We start yoga classes on Tuesday morning,

The exercises are done whilst sitting,

Which does appeal, we don't mind admitting,

For we have a feeling, call it a suspicion,

That we'd never get up from the prone position.

WELL GOOD LUCK
WITH THAT THEN

Look forward, don't look back,
Don't look over your shoulder,
With unbridled ambition your future attack,
Adopt a purpose, think big, be bolder.
That's all very well for youngsters like you,
Oldies like me have a short-term view.

TATTERDEMALION

'Tatterdemalion',
Now there's a word that deserves a medallion,
When last seen
Victoria was Queen,
Investigate it,
Then resuscitate it.

EXISTENTIALISM (2)

If you're a follower of existentialism,
You view life through a pessimistic prism,
If you say you're an existentialist,
You're either depressed or quite possibly pissed,
If you see life as existential,
'Fear and Trembling' [1] are residential.

REPENT

Repent, for the end of the world is nigh,
'Match of the Day' has been suspended,
What can I do but sit here and sigh,
Lamenting the fact that our world is upended?
So what's to blame for this dark mood of mine?
The coronavirus, Covid-one nine.

---

1 A philosophical work by Søren Kierkegaard (1843).

DIES IRAE (2)

How many roles has circumstance bade me play?
And how many have been successful would I say?
Not many,
If any,
That's why sometimes I look so solemn,
It all goes into my debit column.

NO! REALLY?

As a Manxman here in the UK,
It came as a shock to be told today,
So much so, that I needed to be mollified,
On hearing that I had absolutely qualified
(Please, no frivolity)
As a member of an ethnic minority.

SKILLICORN VALLEY

For all you Skillicorns near and far,
Ellan Vannin keeps its doors ajar,
Come wave your flag, state your claim,
Be proud that you've got a Manx family name,
Explore your roots in Skillicorn Valley,
Have your own Skillicorn Rally.

THE RULE OF THREE

To the Rule of Three we are hard-wired,
"Three strikes and you're out"
"Three warnings and you're fired"
And "The Best of Three" is a common shout,
Three examples are generally required,
And Three is Holy, ask the devout.

A REMINDER FOR ME

"Christmas comes but once a year"
Thank the Lord for that,
Switch on your smile, be of good cheer,
Don your Christmas-cracker hat,
Fend off your Christmas blues,
For many would love to be in your shoes.

I'M A MARKED MAN

God knows why and Heaven knows how,
But two lumps have appeared, one each side of my brow,
They're sharp and crusty, like warts or corns,
If I didn't know better, I'd say they were horns,
They're small I agree, but they're definitely growing,
Am I being told it's to Hell that I'm going?

THIS WORRIES ME

These 'horns' on my brow,
Worry me now,
For another link to the diabolical goat
Is the tuft of hair that grows on my throat,
With cloven-hooves and pointed tail,
I'd be the devil's apprentice, doing mischief, to scale.

DREAMS[2]

For Dreams, interpretations of, see Freud,
So Sigmund, tell me, what are they all about?
For last night's dream I thoroughly enjoyed,
You'll say I'm sexually repressed no doubt,
Oh Come On Zigi, this is an expensive wheeze,
In my heart of hearts I know it's due to Cheddar Cheese.

SHOPPING ON LINE

Shopping on line,
You may find fine,
But we don't,
So we won't,
In our dotage we'll drop,
In, God willing, a shop.

---

2. 'Dreams, the topic set by the Great Linford Poetry Group.'

THAT PIGEONS' PERCH
HAS TO GO

Let's not be too hard on them, for they know not what they do,
But our garden and our path are covered in pigeon poo,
This hasn't happened before, maybe they've changed their diet
But unless it stops soon, there's going to be a riot.
I just can't eliminate them, no siree,
So how do I get them to crap from a different tree?

"BRING ME SUNSHINE..."

I hope that I brought my mother some fun,
Long ago when I was young,
God knows, she had enough to sigh about,
And more than enough to cry about
I like to think that just once in a while,
I brought her a laugh, or at least a smile.

RINGING THE BELL

Terry's twelve treatments are finally over,
(That's not to say he's now in the clover),
But his tumor was trapped,
Targeted and zapped,
The staff then gathered to wish him well,
Terry thanked them all, and then, rang the bell.

Jan '20

ON ENTERING A POETRY EXCLUSION ZONE

A poet? Best to keep that quiet,
If asked is that true, best to deny it,
For some will ask, and this is true,
Have you nothing better to do
Than muck around with words,
Poetry, they will tell you, is just for the birds.

BRIGHT AS BELISHA BEACONS

Some bald heads seem burnished bright,
They dazzle with reflected light
Others seem to be French polished,
(For this I stand to be admonished)
But what is it that makes them shine?
And what am I going to do with mine?

THE BULLINGDON CLUB

The Bullingdon Club, the Bullingdon Club,
The future Tory leadership hub,
The nation scoffs
Those Tory Toffs,
That infamous image of arrogant poses,
Our class system it clearly exposes.

COUSIN FRANCES

Every inch a Faragher, I speak of cousin Frances,
All those old photographs she definitely enhances,
Head girl at the Grammar School,
That to me, was pretty cool
Then on to university to gain a BSc,
An example to us all, especially struggling me.

A TEASEL TO TALK ABOUT

You have all seen a teasel, haven't you?
There's one in our garden, well it is Teasel Avenue,
It appeared practically overnight,
And has now reached an incredible height
The neighbours are beginning to talk,
They're only comparing it to Jack's Bean Stalk.

WORRIED? ME?

I have just soaked in a bath of Dr Teal's Epsom Salts,
In the hope that it will banish some of my glaring faults,
Out will go my look of intensity,
I hope that you can grasp the sheer immensity
of this, My groundless looks of angst, will all be corrected,
From now, I will be relaxed, poised, calm and collected.

WOULD YOU BELIEVE IT!

OK guys,
You want a surprise?
I'd sit down if I were you,
It sounds far-fetched but believe me it's true,
I have no wish his name to besmirch,
But it's Eddie Thompson, he's going to church.   Jan '20

ON TRIAL

I stand before you with ego bruised,
For writing smut I stand accused,
That the English language I have abused,
And added to that, you are not amused,
Oh Come On! Relax a little,
Don't be so bloody brittle.

A WHOLE NEW LEXICON

Social distancing, super-spreader, self-isolating,
With all these new phrases my brain is oscillating,
They've replaced the old ones, the ones we know so well,
Like lock-down, confined to barracks, house-arrest,
For three to four months! This is going to test the best,
There may even be a curfew, all together now, BLOODY HELL.

March '20

STANDING UP TO
THE CORONAVIRUS

The latest news is that maybe next week,
The over 70s will be under 'house-arrest',
What will we do, learn Welsh maybe, or Greek?
What a drag, but clearly it will be for the best,
Some Golden Oldies will not be bored,
As sales of Viagra have apparently soared.

"THROUGH FAIR OR
FROSTY WEATHER"

Over this I'm beginning to fret,
Enid and I are prone to forget,
More than that, it's frightening,
It's as if a noose is tightening,
Each other's sentences we have to finish,
But our love for each other it will not diminish.

BEWITCHED

Can we, with any precision,
Determine what decides a decision?
Like, why did he walk the unmarked way?
Prompting others to whisper, "He was led astray,
Under so and so's influence he clearly fell",
Whereas years ago, he'd be under a spell.

A DELICACY (FOR SOME)

Look, I said, don't be a drip,
Listen, I said, get a grip,
Smell it, I said, he held his nose, said it was vile,
Taste it, I said, he said he'd rather run a mile,
Take it, I said, for I sensed a scuffle,
He took it, then threw away my truffle.

"FAT PEOPLE ARE HARDER TO KIDNAP"

Embroided on friend Noel's woollen hat,
"Fat People are Harder to Kidnap,"
It has a certain logic, I will admit to that,
So to avoid the kidnap mishap,
Be obese, rotund, well-fed, whatever,
They will look elsewhere, and you're left feeling clever.

IT'S MAKE YOUR MIND UP TIME

I am a floating voter, yes, a floating voter am I,
I don't know who to vote for and the election's looming nigh,
Previous elections were so easy, vote centre, left or right,

But for this strange election, political theory has taken flight,
It's all about the EU, will we leave or will we remain?
I'll have to hold my nose, for I'm determined not to abstain.

Dec '19

DISSONANCE

Have you heard your own voice? I have, today,
I didn't like the sound of it, not in any way,
The recording, clear to hear,
Wasn't pleasing to my ear,
The lesson therefore, I must deduce,
My verbosity, I must reduce.

FOOD AND SEX

Food and Sex, apparently there is a link,
But what that link might be, I, just cannot think,
An 'insatiable appetite' to both can be applied,
In that there is no doubt, lust and gluttony are implied.
And what about those chocolates, as a gift on special days?
An arrow in the armoury of the Romeos' winning ways?

CURRENTLY ON REMAND

Goats to the left, sheep to the right, [3]
How will I be sorted in 'the dying of the light?' [4]
Once my past has been dissected
To the left I'll be directed,
Whatever will become my lot,
I know it will be bloody hot.

CAPTIVATED

I dared and I looked,
It was then I was hooked
On her warmth and her beauty,
To capture her was clearly my duty.
As to who captured who,
I will leave that to you.

A QUARTET

My word!
Have you heard?
About Peter,
Would you believe it?
Would you Adam and Eve it?
He's only run off with Rita.

---

3. Matthew 25:32-46
4. A phrase in 'Do not go gentle into that good night' by Dylan Thomas.

All along
I knew they were wrong,
About Tim,
Now I can shout,
That without a doubt,
It wasn't him.

He ducked and weaved,
Conned and deceived,
Did Dick
It has reached my ear,
And it's good to hear,
He's now serving ten years in nick.

He's sad and low,
'Cos he's suffered a blow,
Has Dai,
For Siân has left him a note,
And from it I now quote
"I've had a better offer, so good bye".

INFIDELITY [5]

Those sacred cows,

Marriage vows,

Are difficult to keep

The lure of sex

Marriage wrecks,

The betrayed are left to weep.

JUDGES CHAP 16 V 16

I woke up feeling weak,

Still do, as we speak,

And on the floor, around the chair,

Lay several tufts of snow-white hair.

With great effort I managed to stand,

Behind me stood Enid, scissors in hand.

---

5. Infidelity; the topic for the Great Linford Poetry Group, September '19.

IT'S JULY 2020

You may well ask, What's occurring?
For can't you hear the people purring?
Something's happening, something's stirring,
To the Governments guidelines, some are demurring,
But in the main, we are deferring,
As none of us want this lockdown recurring.

ALCOHOL, NARCOTICS, POWER, BEAUTY ETC.

The clue is in the word, hiding in plain sight, [6]
It's the toxic in intoxication,
The poisons in the title offer but a brief delight,
And are but a prelude to a mental devastation,
Seeking the quick thrill, temptation leads us astray,
But an addled brain for the pleasure, is too high a price to pay.

---

6. Based on an essay by Mark Edmundson in 'The Metaphysics of the Hangover.'

WHO OR WHAT INSPIRED YOU TO WRITE?[7]

It's occasionally a 'who' but more often a 'what',
And as to who the 'whos' were, forgive me I've forgot
To say I've been inspired is far too strong a word,
To say my stuff's inspired is blatantly absurd
It is to me an illness with not a cure in sight,
Unless you cut my hands off, these scribbles I will write.

THE DAY AFTER TOMORROW[8]

The day after tomorrow, what can I say about that?
It's three days after yesterday, but keep that under your hat,
Do I read tea-leaves, palms or tarot? No indeed I don't,
Will I forecast the future? No indeed I won't.
I guess, as we're in lockdown, there'll be no change from today,
But I hope that I'm alive to see it, that's all I'm going to say.

---

7. Great Linford Poetry Group's topic for April '20.
8. Great Linford Poetry Group's topic for July '20

LONG ONES

I have no wish to sound imperious,
But from this point on, we're getting serious
There's nothing under six lines here,
So we're playing with the big boys, that's pretty clear.
Seven lines or more,
Gets them through the door.
A word before you enter, don't expect Heroic verse,
Keep in mind that old expression, "Hell yes, it could be worse."

LONG ONES

CONTENTS

"THE MARCH OF TIME"

The Twenty-Twenties start today,
What will they bring? Who can say?

Is it the start of the post-truth era?
Will it bring Armageddon nearer?

Will a war start somewhere? You bet, in a wink
Will we be involved? Huh, what do you think?

Will our vulnerable east coast be drowned?
Will Prince Charles ever be crowned?

Will Tottenham Hotspur win the Premier League
And save their fans from memory fatigue?

Will the Humanities be swamped by science?
Or will somebody, somewhere, lead a defiance?

Through political turmoil and extremes of weather,
Enid and I will face it together.

Will medical science see us through?
Will we be refurbished with organs not quite new?

Will we experience one last adventure
Before falling foul to a form of dementia?

Hopefully, ten years from today, if we survive,
We'll be into our nineties and glad we're alive.

We should think on, as we down our drink,
In the March of Time, ten years is a blink.

January 1st 2020.

AH YES! THE AGEING PROCESS

Two old codgers, Peter, forgetful, and Eddie, hard of hearing,
Were reminiscing, which to Jill, Peter's wife, was quite endearing.
Peter sought, frustratingly, for his hero, Jonathan Miller's name,
Recently deceased, but alas he sought in vain,
"He was a doctor, actor, director, producer but never a critic"
But all that Eddie heard was that magic word 'cricket'
Then heaped upon the great Bob Willis, a garland of praises,
As Peter lauded *his* hero with equally eloquent phrases,
Their cross-wired conversation continued unabated,
Unaware that their heroes were completely unrelated.
Their funny senior moment, they eventually realized,
For Jill it was a treasured moment, a moment to be prized.

Dec '19

SCHOOLDAYS (2)

Beaten was the poor girl, beaten 'till she screamed,
Beaten at her desk until her tears streamed,
Beaten as to the door she fled,
Hands on her ears to protect her head
Impossible were the blows to block,
As we, the class, looked on in shock
Beaten as she ran for the gate,
Every blow with the teacher's full weight,
Blow upon blow on her head she rained,
That sickening sight in my mind has remained.

SAILING STORMY WATERS

Some seem to sail through life
But let us be blunt,
This is just a front
For we're all beset with worries and fears,
But only in private do we shed our tears,
So be kind to all whom we meet on our way,
It restores faith, brings hope and brightens our day.

"SAFE IN THE KNOWLEDGE" (GNOSTICISM AND ME)

Gnosticism could be the ism for me,
Even though it's deemed to be,
By orthodox Christians, heresy.

The perpetual struggle between light and dark,
Gender equality, the Divine Spark,
All, on me, have made a mark.

The knowledge of self, leading to salvation,
Immortality of the soul, the soul's liberation,
Censure by the Orthodox Church, to me, it's validation.

And the tragic fate of the Cathars in France,
The crusades to destroy them and their 'heretical' stance,
Serve to arouse a curiosity and their views to enhance.

Will I, should I, be shunned by the church?
Will they these 'strange' teachings besmirch?
Will they my mind for heresy search?

"NOT ANOTHER ONE"

I've now a second hernia, in the other groin,
That vulnerable point where two muscles join,
The snag is I'm old, the model isn't made anymore,
So repair staff are told to politely ignore,
They will see me as a benign bore, cruelly,
But this must be a design flaw, surely?
Complain to the maker? His response could well appal
What if he orders a product recall?

ALL TOGETHER NOW
"OH DEAR, WHAT CAN
THE MATTER BE..."

In church last Sunday, there was a kerfuffle,
A lady was locked in the loo,
It's a scene that any feathers would ruffle,
The lock wouldn't move, what would she do?

A prayer was said, the Bible read,
But the lock just wouldn't be budged,
"Is there anyone here with enough street-cred
To pick a lock, and not be judged?"

The appeal fell on stony ground,
So who came to her aid but the Fire Brigade,
Three beefy firemen, with haloes crowned,
Rescued the lady, by then at the edges, definitely frayed.

She could have feigned a faint,
Then inwardly glowed, pleased with her scheme,
To be carried out by her helmeted saint,
Which is, it would seem, every woman's erotic dream.

Jan '20

AT LAST I HAVE AN ALLERGY (MAYBE)

I'm not exactly slobbering yet,
But unsolicited saliva
Renders my lower lip wet.

Plus, my lower lip swells
That, along with the bluish tint,
Rings alarming bells.

So kissing is out,
An inevitable consequence
But then again, there's always stout.

But kissing was ever a swapping of spit,
How did it get so popular?
Put like that, it's high time we quit.

"It's something you eat, it's in your diet"
At last I have an allergy,
The doctor could be right, personally, I don't buy it.

Feb '20

YES, BUT IS IT FETCHING?

Is there something you want to tell me, Ed?
It's your lips, they're ruby-red,
What I saw in the mirror gave me a fright,
They are ruby-red, Enid was right
What's worse, they're getting bigger,
(Behind my back I could hear a snigger)
On normal service there will be a pause,
Whilst a medical Sherlock discovers the cause.

March '20

THOUGHTS ON A GERMAN FOLK SONG

I have just come across a translation
(I'll give you one guess at the nation)
Of a philosophical folk song
If you said Germany you wouldn't be wrong.
It's about the freedom of thought,
When I read it, it pulled me up short
It's existentialism, in a German folk song!
Is it possible someone's stringing me along?
But hold on, there is a link,
It's not as strange as I'm prone to think
For Germanic thinkers, back in the day,
In this philosophy, led the way
Heidegger, Tillich and Nietzsche
With Martin Buber also a feature.
There's more to this folk song than meets the eye
I'm anxious to ask who wrote it and why?
This isn't a run of the mill folk song,
But I'll stop here, as I'm probably wrong.

FAQS

If God is dead,
As Nietzsche said,
To what do I pray,
At the end of each day?

Do we have guides
To see us through tides?
Or when push comes to shove
Is it all down to love?

FASHION[9]

Fashion, a capitalist ploy to keep the show on the road,
Spend, spend, consume, lest the system implode
Consumerism keeps the wheels turning,
And fashion helps us prols to keep earning
"That's so very last year dear"
Is stated loudly so we can all hear,
Splash the cash on this year's model,
Which to environmentalists is dangerous twaddle.
Calm down Edward, your bitterness ration,
For socialism is out of fashion.

---

9. Fashion, topic for the month for the Great Linford Poetry Group

DICK BARTON SPECIAL AGENT

That Holy Trinity Dick, Snowy and Jock,
Every night around seven o'clock,
On our 'steam-powered' wireless, they'd be facing death,
Whilst we listened, hooked, with bated breath,
Enthralled,
As their net they trawled,
With crooks and killers securely netted
To the heroic trio we'd feel indebted,
Cliff-hangers every night,
Would they escape their perilous plight?
Of course they did, without shedding blood,
But then, we always knew that they would
Heroes three, enforcing the law,
Against undesirables waging a war.
'Midst my childhood memories, they will always have a place,
Dick Barton, Snowy and Jock, they will always be on the case.

June '19

THESE T-SHIRT SLOGANS

Seen on a T-shirt just this morning:
"Does not play well with others".
Holy Carruthers!
But we understand fully,
He's a must-win bully,
We should thank him for the warning.

But these T–shirt slogans, they're all bespoke,
It wasn't a warning, it was just a joke
So what would I have printed on mine?
Something outrageous, or something benign?
What about a biblical quote, like "Love thy neighbour"?
Or something satirical,
Probably political,
Like, "Bugger this, I'm going to vote Labour".

WHEN SELF-ESTEEM IS IN THE RED ZONE

How do you raise self-esteem?
Help needed, but nothing extreme.
Well, you could read those well meaning annuals,
Those many and oft read, self-help manuals
Or may I whisper in your one good ear
My very own, home-made idea?
Ignore those events that are edged in black,
To answer your question, I wouldn't look back.

MILTON KEYNES, CITY OF DREAMS

Personally speaking,
The title needs tweaking
May I make a suggestion?
Would it read better if put as a question?

'City of Dreams', an engine that pulls railway carriages?
Or a place of fresh starts for middle-aged marriages?
Pedants point out, in prose perfect and pretty,
It has yet to be granted the status of 'City'.

Yes Milton Keynes has many detractors,
But 'Milton Keynes, a place to admire'
Or 'Milton Keynes, a place to inspire'
May fire a search for its positive factors.

Whatever, personally speaking (again), I'm pleased to say,
Fate brought me here and here I will stay.

TO BOLDLY GO

Thinking it a clear-cut no-brainer,
I voted to remain, I became a remainer.
We lost!
There will of course be a cost,
But we'll take it on the chin,
Calling, as we cast off, "let the voyage begin".
Accepting defeat, we hope for the best,
As we boldly go, up and over the crest.

31st January 2020

IT'S HAIR, BUT NOT AS WE KNOW IT

A tuft of hair has mysteriously appeared,
It's long, grey and wispy, in fact it looks weird
It's in an unusual place,
Not on my head, chest or face,
But at the base of my throat, above my shirt,
And, I might add, it's far from inert
As it grows profusely,
It could be ornamental, (I use the term loosely)
To this tuft I'm attached, of course,
If you want to remove it you'll have to use force.

June '20

A SONG TOO FAR

I am prepared to wager,
That no ex-sergeant-major,
Is somewhere singing the following:
"With a hey and a ho and a hey nonny no,
When birds do sing, hey ding a ding ding",
But I am, and it takes some swallowing.

Old Comrades will think
That I'm now wearing pink,

They would take the Michael,

Say I've gone full cycle,

And I have to admit,

It just doesn't fit,

So to quell any doubt,

I shall sit this one out.

MY WORST DECISION[10]

This will be short as I mustn't bore,

But back in nineteen ninety-four,

As always, in a manner most irrational,

We backed four horses in the National

Enid backed Minneloma, Freddie Starr's horse,

But at the bookies, this bet I wouldn't endorse,

It was a decision I try hard to forget,

For Minneloma won, much to my regret.

Enid watched the race at home and eagerly awaited

My arrival with the winnings, but was devastated,

For I was empty-handed, winnings had I none,

I had to do some grovelling, either that or run.

---

10. Great Linford Poetry Group's topic for July.

STRANGER THAN FICTION

People stop and stare at this most unusual sight,
It's like a suitcase on six wheels,
Rounded, no sharp corners, antenna, coloured white.

It's a seemingly unaided travelling case,
It's the strangeness that appeals,
Silently travelling along at a gentle walking pace.

They're employed by the Co-op store, it's said,
Delivering ingredients for meals
No vans or drivers for them then, compliant robots instead.

Seeing one initially, you'd think you'd lost the plot,
Supplying this robotic service, an easy search reveals,
Are Starship Deliveries MK, futuristic or what?

June '20

A PLAN DISRUPTED[11]

There were no plans of mine to be thwarted,
But a plan of my grandfather's was hung drawn and quartered.
A mother's love ruined his intention,
Lives were changed by her intervention.
For those involved, it was surely a dramatic event,
As hearts and relationships were irreparably rent.

Rhyme will be briefer than prose,
So this is how the story goes.

In nineteen hundred and four, the drama came to a head,
Before I could question them, the protagonists were dead.
Wil Haydn Davies, landlord of the Machno Inn,
Married to 'Sal Machno', had an affair with helper Nin.
This illicit liaison (think of the scandal) produced a child,
Mabel Parry Jones, born out of wedlock, by chapel defiled.
Challenging the fates,
Wil set sail for the States
In finding a job and a house, he proved more than able,
He was set to forge a new life, for himself, Sal and Mabel.
The event peaked in Liverpool, on the Landing Stage,

11. "A plan that had to be changed and why". The topic for the Great Linford
Poetry group meeting, August 2019.

Sal and Mabel were boarding the ship when Nin arrived
in a rage

Grabbing Mabel, she said to the police, in a voice defiant
and clear,
"She is MY daughter and she's staying here."
Imagine the scene; Mabel pulled from one to another,
Sal sailed without Mabel, who later became my mother.
Of course, as with any story, 'What ifs' abound,
And if Nin had been late arriving, I wouldn't be around.

July '19

IT'S THE SINGING[12]

My favourite TV programme? No I don't have one,
But I do like, 'Dechrau Canu, Dechrau Canmol',
(Start singing, start praising), DC DC for short,
On S4C, 7:30 every Sunday.

It's hymn singing from non-conformist chapels such as
Bethania, the Wesleyan chapel in Bryn-y-Maen,
Or Salem, the Calvinist chapel in Maes-y-Bont,
Or Hebron, the Baptist chapel in Tyn-y-Groes.

---

12. 'Your Favourite TV or Radio Show' Topic for the Great Linford Poetry
Group Feb '20

It's the singing, heads up, shoulders back, mouths open,
Enjoyment and enthusiasm by the shedload,
Old favourites by William Williams Pantycelyn,
Altos, Sops, Basses, Tenors, all are clearly heard.

On every programme the chapels are full,
Some may be there to be seen on TV,
So what? It's a chance to sing, that's the pull,
They know, they know, that it sets the mind free.

A SIGNPOST WOULD HELP

So, I ask, is there a meaning to my life?
It's a question asked by many, it's a question that is rife,
If there is, it's proving hard to find,
So go ahead and tell me that I'm spiritually blind.

What about a purpose, that should be easier to see,
You'd think it would be, yes, with that I will agree
But no, I can't see a purpose either,
Am I then a hopeless case, seemingly with neither?

Of course they may be hidden, not for me to know,
So I may well be living them, in my status quo
Or again, they may not even exist,
That's the bookies' favourite, and yes, I get their gist.

Yes, you're all at sea Edward but you can be brought ashore,
There is a way, if you want, a way you shouldn't ignore,
It'll get you into harbour, home, dry and safe,
Do what many others do, find yourself a faith.

But what should I have faith in, can I pick and choose?
Is there a catalogue which I can peruse?
Edward, open up your mind, the choice is yours to make,
You life is at a crossroads, you know which road to take.

April '20

CITY OF DREAMS

'City of Dreams' is a reference to an ethereal urban development
Where needs and wants are met,
Where hopes and aspirations can be fulfilled,
Where altruism rules,
Where tolerance of difference is observed,
Where the crime rate is nil,
Where entrepreneurial spirit and labour are justly rewarded,
Where equality exists.
Can you see a society, past, present or future, coming even close?
No, neither can I,
So let's confine the term 'City of Dreams'
To cruise liners and railway engines.

MY IDEAL DAY[13]

To lighten their load,
As they travel their road,
To help them on their way,
That would be a feel-good day.

To lift them up when they are down,
To raise a laugh, replace a frown,
To keep despondency at bay,
That would be a worthwhile day.

To see them smile,
On their final mile,
To find encouraging words to say,
That would be my ideal day.

---

13. My Ideal Day, topic for the Great Linford Poetry Group Feb 2020

IN PRAISE OF 'X'

The letter X earns its pay,
Given the roles it has to play,
To write it off is reprehensible,
For to symbolism it is indispensable.

It marks the spot, and tells us we're wrong,
Signifies a vote, acts as a certificate,
Sends a kiss, counts as ten and instructs us to multiply,
Represents the unknown (e.g. in algebraic equations).

It symbolizes Christ and Christianity,
Serves as a signature for the illiterate,
Informs us of extra-large clothing sizes (XL),
Denotes a chromosome.

It reveals the times that alcohol has been distilled (XXX),
Flags up all things experimental, (X-type Jaguar),
Notifies dishonesty, (the double cross),
Abbreviates Christmas (Xmas).

Should you ever view X as expendable,
Please be aware, it's extremely bendable,
And yes, in our lexis it's infrequently used,
But given its roles elsewhere, this can be excused.

MARCEL PROUST (1871-1922)

Novelist Marcel Proust explored memory and perception,
He saw memory as an enigma, and the necessity of reflection
The dominant time in the human condition, is, he said, the past,
We are all essentially nostalgic, and our mental archives vast
It's a fact, he claimed, that at times we may regret,
That the past we are obviously unable to forget.

Voluntary memory needs a conscious effort to recall,
Involuntary memory needs no such effort at all,
With Proust it was the taste of a Madeleine biscuit
dipped in tea,
His grandmother's favourite snack, that would set his
memory free.

But my unsought memories seem to appear at will,
Place, face or event, from the ether they spill,
No trigger required,
He was right of course, to our past we're hard-wired.

LOST AND REGAINED

Ned Maddrell died in nineteen seventy-four,
Of native Manx speakers, the last,
On our Celtic culture this closed the door,
Another language confined to the past.

But wait, it isn't so,
For conversations in Manx were recorded,
A debt to enthusiasts we definitely owe,
Their efforts to preserve it are here applauded.

Manx is now enjoying a revival,
These new speakers should receive an award,
Against the odds they've ensured its survival,
Part of our heritage they have restored.

THERE'S NOTHING LIKE A
GOOD MOAN

Who would have thought,
After all those countries, regions and addresses
I would end up here in MK,
The Goddess Fortuna is having her way.
But I haven't exactly 'ended up', not quite, not yet,
Five years more, max,

Maybe six, if I learn to relax,

There's another depressing fact,

Most of those that I meet or see

Are many years younger than me,

So my clock is ticking loudly.

Still, as a Stoic would say,

In an earnest yet encouraging way,

"Shit happens, get over it".

"BRITISH NATURISM IS SEEING AN UPSWING IN MEMBERS"

"British Naturism is seeing an upswing in members."
Do we need to know this?[14]

They'll see a downturn in December,

When Old Jack Frost strikes hard.

Joking aside,

They will all do well to remember,

That members' upswings are barred.

---

14. Letter by Andrew Kay via the times.co.uk in The Sunday Times Travel Supplement 8.7.18

LIFE UNDER 'HOUSE ARREST' (WEEK 1)

Following these, so far semi-enforced, Government guidelines,
Almost everything is closing down (including people)
This frees up time, no need now to keep one eye on the clock,
In a way it echoes childhood, when we had so much time,
And the old saying "Time enough" was on peoples' lips
How long the day seems, now that time has lost its importance
But follow the guide lines we must, for these are troubled times,
A Tsunami of death, COVID-19, without doubt, primes.

WEEK 1 (CONTD.)

Do it now, self-isolate,
Or if you like, self-insulate,
Whatever, but please, society serve,
Do your bit to flatten the curve,
Do it now don't hesitate.

March '20

LIFE UNDER 'HOUSE ARREST' (WEEK 2)

Standards are slipping,
This just isn't me, watching daytime TV,
The bird bath needs cleaning, tomorrow, maybe,
I'm wearing odd socks and shave twice a week,
I'm still in bed and it's ten as we speak.
Standards are definitely slipping.

WEEK 2 (CONTD.)

This house arrest gives me time to ponder,
It gives my mind time to wander,
I will never forget,
And may live to regret,
All this time I'm about to squander.   March '20

LIFE UNDER 'HOUSE ARREST' (WEEK 3)

How did Terry Waite survive,
Those four years, or was it five,
In solitary confinement in Beirut?

To him, this 'house arrest' is just a hoot,

So come on Ed, get a grip,

Compared to his experience, this is a mere blip.

WEEK 3 (CONTD.)

At the Government's wise insistence,

I will keep a social distance,

But at their behest,

I'm in house arrest,

It doesn't apply in a domestic existence.

April '20

LIFE UNDER 'HOUSE ARREST' (WEEK 4)

My life is now lived in virtuality,

Some others live in a virtual reality,

This coronavirus is not convivial,

Radically decreasing conviviality

Worse than that, its behaviour is brutal,

It's seeing us off with a shocking brutality.

WEEK 4 (CONTD.)

Standards continue to slip,
It's time I was getting a grip,
My body and brain are reclining,
To be busy they're simply declining,
This lockdown is more than a blip.

April '20

LIFE UNDER 'HOUSE ARREST' (WEEK 5)

Following Government guidelines and death-toll data,
We can't help feeling that sooner or later,
We'll fall to this virus as around the globe it rages,
This Covid-19, this slayer of all ages,
If we survive,
And at the end of the tunnel safely arrive,
For the many acts of kindness, we hope to have latitude,
Time and opportunity in which to show our gratitude.
They serve to remind us, as if we need to be told,
That at 85 and 83, we are utterly, totally, without doubt, old.

WEEK 5 (CONTD.)

Enid and I are on an assignment,
We've been told to enter domestic confinement,
So there we have it, we're self-isolating,
From the world outside we're dislocating,
From our social life it's an early retirement.

April '20

LIFE UNDER 'HOUSE ARREST' (WEEK 6)

Who'd have thought that this pesky little virus
Would so desperately desire us
So to kill us with impunity,
As no one has immunity.
It has brought the world to its knees,
Riding along on a cough or a sneeze.

WEEK 6 (CONTD.)

Dear Diary, 6th week adrift and still no sight of land,
The crew have eaten the Captain; things are getting out of hand,
At least, for now, we are alive,
But how, like this, will we survive?
Looking on the bright side, we are all nicely tanned.

April '20

LIFE UNDER 'HOUSE ARREST' (WEEK 7)

We're staggering into the seventh week
'Midst a total, global nightmare,
People are dying as we speak,
This virus is laying our world's plight bare,
We're moving towards an unknown destination,
Increasingly doubtful of a restoration.

WEEK 7 (CONTD.)

You self-contained people may scoff,
But week seven is pissing me off
Yet among the things in our favour,
This one we dearly savour,
We've yet to develop that dreaded cough.   April '20

LIFE UNDER 'HOUSE ARREST' (WEEK 8)

Week 8 and counting, I doubt this is going to end,
I'm keeping calm with camomile tea,
Without it I'd go 'round the bend.
Family, friends and the 'phone, for help hold the key,
But wait, Boris is back, and talking of easing the brakes,
And still, he assures us, determined to do what it takes.

WEEK 8 (CONTD.)

Sitting on the 'Throne' aids concentration,
I find it conducive to contemplation,
Of toilet paper we've one roll left,
Panic buying has left us bereft,
To use both sides brings consternation.

April '20

LIFE UNDER 'HOUSE ARREST' (WEEK 9)

There's a whiff of cautious optimism about,
As there's talk of a road map to get us out
Of course the virus is still on the loose,

So let's not put our heads in a noose,
Let's keep in mind there's a killer out there,
Let's play it safe, we need to take care.

WEEK 9 (CONTD.)

It's a whacky idea for Covid protection,
Thankfully laughed out of contention,
Should you find yourself infected,
With Jeyes Fluid be injected,
For all the wrong reasons, it attracts our attention.

May '20

LIFE UNDER 'HOUSE ARREST' (WEEK 10)

Let's face it, we're up the creek,
Without a paddle, so to speak
Some of us snuggle up, safely in the boat,
Others, in the water, struggle to stay afloat,
But let us look on the bright side,
Tomorrow there will be a high tide
That will carry us onto a sandy shore,
There to pick up our lives once more.

WEEK 10 (CONTD.)

To all key workers raise our praises,

Their dedication to their work amazes,

Reward their attitude,

Show our gratitude,

Double their wages, now, not in stages.   May '20

LIFE UNDER 'HOUSE ARREST' (WEEK 11)

Social groups are stirring,

Hosts are up and purring,

Members too are itching,

To return to their twitching or stitching,

They will still keep six feet apart (I never did go metric),

But they will meet up with each other, and enjoy the rhetoric.

For society to be open, we will have to wait,

Then in church, pub and restaurant, we will celebrate.

WEEK 11 (CONTD.)

Week eleven and ahead there is a light,
To our unplanned voyage the end is in sight,
So we'll, "Bend to the oar"
And "Pull for the shore"
But we fear this won't be the end of our plight.

May '20

LIFE UNDER 'HOUSE ARREST' (WEEK 12)

We've made it, we're safely tied up in harbour,
But we face restrictions on going ashore,
We're in dire need of a pint and a barber,
But the harbour master we can't ignore,
With rations ferried in, it should be far from bleak,
So OK, we'll stay tied up, for just another week.

WEEK 12 (CONTD.)

From coast to coast come one, come all,
Be upstanding for this toast I call,
To our key workers, what a team
With which to confront Covid nineteen,
To that noble workforce, who can now walk tall.

To our key workers.   May '20

LIFE UNDER 'HOUSE ARREST' (WEEK 13)

I've got to stop writing this stuff,
My inner voice cries, enough is enough
This lockdown could go on for ages,
This is just one of the prelim stages.
It's week thirteen and a weariness shows,
So from now on, I will stick to prose.

WEEK 13 (CONTD.)

A confession, on Sunday I had the gall
Yes the temerity, to go over the wall,
What a joy, what a caper,
To go and buy a Sunday paper,
But better by far, was feeling free, walking tall.

June '20

ASSESSMENTS

To assess, rate, review,
Is an incredibly difficult thing to do
To size up, weigh up, measure,
What to someone is an absolute treasure
To examine, evaluate, judge

Is a hard task that no one should fudge,
Constructive criticism and reassuring praise
Needs courage, skill and learning, in many different ways,
Always the aim must be to foster, fuel, foment,
To encourage, always, that must be the intent.

WARNING, BE AWARE

As we wend and weave our way
Through this hazardous minefield of life,
We should tread very carefully,
As the potential for loss is rife.

To retrieve lost core-values (let's call them 'properties'),
Is always a difficult task,
As there is no 'Lost Property' office,
It's almost an impossible ask.

Losing any of our 'properties' invokes a terrible cost,
So what are these personal properties, that are so easily lost?

Reputation, Freedom, Hope,
Sanity, 'Our way', Faith,
Confidence, Interest, Trust,
'The Will', Rights and Privileges.
Of course this is not an exhaustive list,
For I've lost my thread, but you get the gist.

MY WATERLOO

Just before the break of day,

My waterworks will have their way

From my sleep it does disturb me,

Yes you're right, it does perturb me.

From my bed I will arise,

Crusty sleep still in my eyes,

Every night with routine true,

My bladder brings me to the loo.

SCHOOLDAYS (3)

Latin lessons with Miss Isles

Did not elicit many smiles

They did instead, threaten detentions,

For not knowing those boring declensions.

Revenge was the aim

Of this pun on her name,

"We'd throw missiles to the lions".

THE FLEET REVIEW

Walking along the Grand Union Canal yesterday,
We spotted a formidable fleet of Canada Geese,
It looked like a fleet review, so I stopped and saluted,
They were probably on patrol, sort of, keeping the peace.

Full ahead steamed the forward screen,
Eight in total, in arrowhead formation,
With Mother Goose as Flag Ship,
Ensuring they kept to their station.

Following them came the convoy,
Eighteen, in close disciplined pairs, steaming line ahead,
Adult male, head up, sailing point,
Adult female, sailing aft; both displaying parent-cred.

It was an impressive sight,
Such style and seemingly effortless grace,
Such a visual delight
That to toast them at home, I spliced the mainbrace.

THE VIEW FROM THE TOWPATH

These narrowboat crews
Enjoy their cruise,
Chugging along at a leisurely pace
With a calm serenity and elegant grace.

I envy their 'nautical' skills,
And their lack of need of sea-sickness pills,
With Captain Birds Eye at the helm,
They seem to be entering a different realm.

They glide slowly by, almost sedately,
And give us a wave, almost stately
All those aboard look so content,
It looks like a life style heaven-sent.

EDDIE THOMPSON

WE'RE FOLLOWING THE GOVERNMENT'S GUIDELINES

Hugs are out, kisses too,

So how are we to show pleasure at a visit from you?

Hand-shakes and high fives, all are forbidden,

So our joy at seeing you will have to stay hidden.

You stand on the path at the right social distance,

Six feet apart, at the Government's insistence,

Whilst we stand in the doorway to have a chat

About how we all are, and this and that.

We'd sooner sit down with tea and a biscuit,

 But the way things are, we'd rather not risk it

It's our families and friends who inspire us,

To do our bit to defeat this virus.

LONGER ONES

I know what you're going to say,
Longer Ones are a bore,
Like waiting for Norwich City to score,
So to keep your looming boredom at bay,
And thinking specifically of you,
I have kept them down to a reasonable two.

LONGER ONES

CONTENTS

THE ZOOMED READING

The Zoom church service this morning,
Dragged me unwillingly,
Into something I see chillingly,
But sold to me a new age dawning.

It pushed my blood pressure off the gauge,
It was being on stage without a rehearsal,
I still can't relax, long after dispersal,
"Get used to it; Zoom will soon be the rage".

Enid trimmed my nose hair,
And my trusty jumper I shed,
A mist descended, tainted red,
A hint of panic was in the air.

Siting the tablet caused a kerfuffle,
"Too close, too far, too high, too low",
"And those hairs in your nose will definitely show."
The prep, the build-up, my feathers did ruffle.

"I'm on" I said, then missed my cue,
That this could happen I'd clearly foreseen,
Acts chapter one, verses six to fourteen,
It was over, fini, I'd blown it and knew.

We followed the service, me ashamed,
When another cue came along,
Another chance, I'm still in, I was wrong,
A big breath and my voice to the tablet I aimed.

My reading I tentatively entered,
Were we in view? Could I be heard?
I tried to enunciate every word,
Just for a moment my attention was centred.

Tonight I'll have a Guinness or two,
Tomorrow I'll keep my head down,
In case it's asked around in town,
Who gave that reading? Eddie who?

May '20

HOW IT WAS (1): LAYING AND LIGHTING THE FIRE[15]

1. Fill one bucket with coal, another with slack.
    (The 'coal-hole' was outside, 'out the back'.)

2. Rake out ashes from previous fire.
    (The worst part of the job, mucky, dire.)

3. Crumple paper and place in grate.
    (Copies of the Daily Graphic, couldn't dawdle,
    work at eight.)

4. Place sticks, from oven, on paper, criss-crossed.
    (Criss-crossed mind, not just tossed.)

5. Place coal on sticks.
    (You can see why I got up at six.)

6. Ensure damper is 'OUT'.
    (Followed the drill like a good boy-scout.)

7. Set paper alight.
    (No time to see if sticks ignite.)

8. Hold paper across flue, helping fire to 'draw'.
    (There was always a draught, you could hear the roar.)

---

15. Fire, the month's topic for the poetry group, November 2019.

9.   Once fire takes, push damper 'IN'.
     (At this stage you would feel that you could win.)

10. Place guard in front of fire.
     (Important this, sparks could start a funeral pyre.)

11. Clean the hearth, brush up dust.
     (Ship-shape and Bristol fashion, this was a must.)

12. Refill coal bucket.
     (If the fire didn't 'take', I'd cuss with a phrase I
     can't use here.)

                                                    Oct '19

EPILOGUE

This is the last word, the 'in addition', the postscript,
As I'm off, boots, scarf and hat on, jacket zipped
I hope you've enjoyed the last half-hour
With my verses Sweet and Sour,
If you did, I'm Eddie Thompson,
If you didn't, I'm Hedy Compton.

BV - #0073 - 231120 - C0 - 203/127/7 - PB - 9781861519689 - Gloss Lamination